Berlin im Glanz der Nacht *Berlin after Dusk*

DETLEF BLUHM

BERLIN IM GLANZ DER NACHT

Berlin after Dusk

be.bra verlag

Bibliografische Information der Deutschen Nationalbibliothek
Die Deutsche Nationalbibliothek verzeichnet diese Publikation in der Deutschen Nationalbibliografie; detaillierte bibliografische Daten sind im Internet über http://dnb.d-nb.de abrufbar.

KulturBrauerei Haus 2
Schönhauser Allee 37, 10435 Berlin
post@bebraverlag.de
Lektorat: Robert Zagolla, Berlin
Englische Übersetzung: Penny Croucher, London
Umschlag & Satz: typegerecht, Berlin
Schrift: Seravek
Druck und Bindung: Finidr, Český Těšín
ISBN 978-3-89809-155-8

www.bebraverlag.de

VORWORT

»In der Nacht bloß zu schlafen hieße die Sache nicht ernst zu nehmen.«
Douglas Adams, ***Der lange dunkle Fünfuhrtee der Seele***

Sind wir Fotografen Jäger? Wenn wir Fotos schießen, ein Motiv gut treffen, eine Situation richtig eingefangen haben oder auf Foto-Safari gehen? Mich hat schon immer die umgangssprachliche Anwendung der Terminologie des Waidwerks auf das Handwerk des Fotografen gewundert. Obwohl ... die Spezies der Paparazzi besteht ja vor allem aus Jägern, die auch gern in der Nacht jagen. Manchmal sogar mit tragischen Folgen.

Aber nein, ich empfinde mich nicht als Jäger, auch wenn ich auf meinen nächtlichen Streifzügen durch Berlin manchmal das Gefühl hatte, auf der Pirsch zu sein. Deren Erfolg hängt ja bekanntlich davon ab, ob man zur richtigen Zeit am richtigen Ort auftaucht. So geschehen bei meinem Foto vom Haus der Kulturen der Welt (Seite 56/57). Als ich dort ankam, spiegelte sich das Gebäude bei fast vollständiger Windstille nahezu perfekt in seinem vorgelagerten Wasserbecken. Leider stand ein großer Reisebus neben dem Eingang, um den sich viele Menschen tummelten. Doch als ich mein Stativ aufgebaut und die Kamera eingerichtet hatte, stiegen alle ein. Der Bus fuhr kurz darauf ab, und ich konnte in Ruhe mein Bild machen. Kaum fertig, kam der Bus zurück und seine Insassen stiegen wieder aus. Ich hatte Glück gehabt, befand mich zur richtigen Zeit am richtigen Ort.

Auf jeder nächtlichen Exkursion habe ich einen Plan, eine Vorstellung, welche Objekte ich fotografieren möchte – zur ersten Orientierung sehe ich mir meine Motive vorher tagsüber an. Aber manchmal entdecke ich zufällig Perspektiven, die so nicht auf meinem Zettel stehen. So zum Beispiel, als ich gerade einige Motive in der Karl-Marx-Allee aufgenommen hatte und mit meinem Fahrrad zum Ostbahnhof fuhr, um mit der S-Bahn den Heimweg anzutreten. Am Bahnhof angelangt musste ich feststellen, dass die nächtliche

FOREWORD

'Merely sleeping overnight was not taking the business seriously'
Douglas Adams, *The Long Dark Teatime of the Soul*

When we photographers shoot our images, hit on a good subject, capture a situation perfectly or go on a photo-safari – can we be compared with hunters? It has always surprised me that the colloquial terminology of the chase is applied to the photographer's craft. Although ... the Paparazzi species of photographer certainly consists mainly of hunters who also enjoy hunting at night. Sometimes even with tragic consequences.

But no, I don't see myself as a hunter, even if on my nocturnal forays through Berlin I may sometimes get the feeling that I am out stalking. Of course, the success of these forays depends on whether I turn up in the right place at the right time – as happened with my photo of the House of World Cultures (page 56/57). When I arrived there, there was almost no wind at all and the reflection of the building in the water in front of it was close to perfection. Unfortunately, a large tourist coach was standing next to the entrance and lots of people were swarming around it. But after I had set up my tripod and organised my camera, they all got in the coach. The coach drove off shortly afterwards and I was able to take my picture in peace. I had just finished when the coach returned, and its passengers got out again. I had been lucky and found myself in the right place at the right time.

On every nocturnal outing I have a plan, an idea of what I'd like to photograph and for initial orientation I look at my subjects beforehand by day. But sometimes, I accidentally discover perspectives that weren't on my list. Like in August, for example. I had just taken some pictures in Karl-Marx-Allee and cycled to the Ostbahnhof to get the S-Bahn train home. When I got to the station I realised that at night the trains stopped earlier than I had thought; the last S-Bahn left before my very eyes and I had to cycle about

Bereitstellung des öffentlichen Nahverkehrs früher endete als von mir vermutet: Die letzte S-Bahn war mir vor der Nase weggefahren, und ich musste die knapp zehn Kilometer bis zu meiner Wohnung mit dem Fahrrad zurücklegen. Dabei entdeckte ich als Bildmotiv die Aral-Tankstelle in der Holzmarktstraße (Seite 166), den Blick von der Mühlendammbrücke auf den Berliner Dom (Buchcover und Seite 149) und die Spittelkolonnaden in der Leipziger Straße (Seite 119). So entstanden auf meinem Heimweg drei Fotografien, an die ich bis dahin gar nicht gedacht hatte. Als ich schließlich in der Morgendämmerung nach Hause kam, war ich heilfroh, die letzte S-Bahn verpasst zu haben. Auch wenn ich finde, dass die Stadt, die gern als Metropole bezeichnet wird, auf ihr vielgepriesenes Nachtleben zumindest verkehrstechnisch noch nicht optimal eingestellt ist.

Das Wort Nachtleben verdankt die deutsche Sprache übrigens ausgerechnet einem Pietisten: dem Schriftsteller, Journalisten und Übersetzer Philipp Balthasar Sinold (1657–1742). Es war im Zeitalter des Barock, als man – an den königlichen und fürstlichen Höfen – die künstlich erhellte Nacht zum Tag werden ließ. Feuerwerke und Theateraufführungen, Musikdarbietungen, Tanzvergnügen, Maskenbälle und Gartenfeste – die Nacht wurde wie nie zuvor mit Genuss und Leben gefüllt. Nicht lange danach leuchtete es auch in den bürgerlichen Quartieren hell und schließlich immer heller.

Die im neunzehnten und frühen zwanzigsten Jahrhundert durch neue Technologien in Gang gesetzte Beleuchtung der Stadt wurde von Anbeginn fotografisch begleitet. Zahllose Fotografen waren fasziniert davon, Stadtlandschaften auf Nachtbildern sichtbar zu machen – eine Möglichkeit, die zuvor dem Gemälde, der Zeichnung, dem Kupferstich oder dem Holzschnitt vorbehalten war. Die Nachtfotografie erlebte eine Blütezeit bis zu ihrem Höhepunkt in der Weimarer Republik. Die vermutlich umfangreichste Serie von über einhundert Berliner Nachtfotografien in dieser Zeit stammt aus dem Jahr 1928, aufgenommen von einem unbekannten Fotografen. Die Bilder zeigen unter anderem das legendäre Haus Vaterland am Potsdamer Platz, das Kino Titania Palast in der Steglitzer Schloßstraße, das Vergnügungs-Etablissement Europa Tanz Pavillon am Anhalter Bahnhof und die Tanzpaläste Florida und Columbia am Kurfürstendamm. Im sogenannten Dritten Reich reglementierten die Nationalsozialisten nicht nur die Tanz- und Musikstile in den Nachtlokalen (»Swing tanzen verboten«), sondern auch deren fotografische Aufnahmen. Nachtfotos waren verpönt. Die Nachtfotografie hat sich

10 kilometres back to my flat. In doing so, I discovered the image of the Aral service station (page 166), the view from the Muehlendammbruecke of the Berlin Cathedral (book cover and page 149) and the Spittel Colonnades in Leipziger Strasse (page 119). So, on my way home I took three photos that I had never thought of before then.

When I finally reached my flat at dawn, I was delighted that I had missed the last S-Bahn – even though I feel that a city that likes to be called a metropolis and has a much-vaunted nightlife, is not best served by its public transport system.

Incidentally, the German language has the Pietist writer, journalist and translator Philipp Balthasar Sinold (1657-1742) to thank for the word 'Nachtleben' (nightlife). During the baroque era the royal courts used artificial light to turn night into day. Firework displays and theatrical performances, musical presentations, dances, masked balls and garden parties – the nights had never been filled with such enjoyment and life. It wasn't long before bourgeois homes shone with light as well, eventually more and more brightly. Then, in the 19th and early 20th Century when new technologies brought in street lighting, photographic records were kept right from the start. Countless photographers were fascinated by making city landscapes visible on pictures taken at night – something that had previously only been possible in paintings, drawings, etchings or wood-carvings.

Night photography flourished and had its heyday in the Weimar Republic; probably the most extensive series of over one hundred night photographs of Berlin was taken by an unknown photographer in 1928. Among them are pictures of the legendary Haus Vaterland on Potsdamer Platz, the Titania Palast cinema in Schlossstrasse Steglitz, the Europa Tanz Pavillon entertainment venue at Anhalter Station and the Florida and Columbia dance halls on the Kurfuerstendamm. In the so-called Third Reich, the National Socialists not only regulated the styles of dance and music in the night clubs ('Swing Dance is Prohibited') but also any photographs taken in them. Night photos were taboo. Even today night photography hasn't completely recovered from this verdict; it still leads a shadowy existence.

Jean Cocteau once aptly remarked: "At night one sees a town exactly as it is". The different intensity of its illumination – from the splendidly-lit

Kaiser-Wilhelm-Gedächtniskirche | Charlottenburg

Kaiser Wilhelm Memorial Church | Charlottenburg district

von diesem Verdikt bis heute nicht endgültig erholt. Sie führt nach wie vor ein Schattendasein.

»Wie eine Stadt gemacht ist, sieht man am besten zur Nachtzeit«, hat Jean Cocteau einmal treffend angemerkt. Die unterschiedliche Intensität ihrer Illumination – vom prächtig erleuchteten Boulevard bis zum mondbeschienenen Stadtwald – erzeugt zahllose Varianten der Schattierung ihres Antlitzes. In unserer Sprache aber haben die unterschiedlichsten Nacht-Kontraste im Vergleich zur eher homogenen Tagesansicht der Stadt keine adäquate Entsprechung. Im Gegenteil. Darauf jedenfalls hat der Schriftsteller Elias Canetti hingewiesen: »Die Tage werden unterschieden, aber die Nacht hat einen einzigen Namen«. Wie als Antwort darauf hat der französische Literat Michel Tournier in seinem Roman »Zwillingssterne« eine Hymne auf die Nacht formuliert: »Das Dunkel löscht den Dreck, das Hässliche, das üppige Wuchern der Mittelmäßigkeit aus. Die spärlichen, schwachen, engumkränzten Lichter entreißen der Nacht ein Stück Hauswand, einen Baum, eine schattenhafte Gestalt, ein Gesicht, all das jedoch aufs äußerste vereinfacht, stilisiert, auf seine Quintessenz verdichtet«.

Die Geringschätzung der Nacht, auf die neben den Genannten viele andere Künstler immer wieder aufmerksam gemacht haben, spiegelt sich auch in der Redewendung »Hässlich wie die Nacht« wider. Sicherlich spielt hierbei unser genetisches Gepäck aus früheren Zeiten eine gewichtige Rolle. Auch nach der Beherrschung des Feuers blieb die Nacht für uns Menschen eine bedrohliche Zeit, ein Raum der Ungewissheit. Jenseits der Sphäre des Hellen lauert auch für uns Heutige immer noch ein tief empfundenes Unbehagen.

In seinem Zyklus »Beneath the Roses« porträtiert der amerikanische Fotograf Gregory Crewdson die amerikanische Provinz. Seine perfekt inszenierten, ans Surreale grenzenden Fotografien sind während der Dämmerung oder in der Nacht aufgenommen. Auf jedem Bild ist mindestens ein Mensch zu sehen, manchmal mehrere, nie aber Gruppen. Bei einigen Fotos sieht man sie erst auf den zweiten Blick. In meinen Fotografien wird man Menschen vergeblich suchen. Die Darstellung menschlicher Einsamkeit auf der Folie nächtlicher Ansichten ist nicht mein Thema. In meinen Nachtbildern sind die Ansichten von Straßen und Plätzen, Gebäuden und Monumenten, Innen-

boulevards to the moonlit urban woods – produces innumerable variations of shadows on its face. But in our language the very varied night contrasts have no adequate equivalent in comparison with its rather more uniform countenance during the day. Quite the opposite; the writer Elias Canetti, at any rate, pointed this out: "The days are different, but the night has a single name". As if in reply, the French writer Michel Tournier composed a Hymn to the Night in his novel *Gemini:*

"The darkness effaces the dirt, the ugliness, the teeming mediocrity of it all. Occasionally a fleeting pool of light snatches a wall, a tree, a figure or a face out of the night, but all simplified in the extreme, stylized, pared to essentials, a house reduced to an architectural design, a tree to a spectral hatch, a face to an isolated outline."

The contempt for the night that is shown again and again by many other artists, as well as those mentioned, is reflected in the German saying *Hässlich wie die Nacht* ('ugly as the night'). Our genetic baggage from earlier times is undoubtedly playing a strong role here. Even after humans had learnt to control fire, the night remained a threatening time for us, a place of uncertainty. Beyond the sphere of lightness there still remains for us today a deep sense of unease.

In his photographic series *Beneath the Roses* the American photographer Gregory Crewdson portrays the American countryside. Bordering on the surreal, his perfectly-composed pictures were taken at dusk or at night. In each photograph there is at least one person, sometimes several, but never groups. In some pictures you only notice them when you take a second look.

In my photographs you will search in vain for any people at all. Depicting human loneliness against a background of nocturnal views is not my area of interest. In my night photos the views of streets and squares, buildings and monuments, interiors and parks, sports grounds and traffc junctions, sacred buildings and cemeteries, are devoid of people.

When the blue hour is long past and astronomical twilight wields the sceptre, everything in the city is still. Occasionally, there are voices between the rows of buildings and on the main roads taxis collect up the last revellers. Then other sounds reach our ears. In the Tiergarten the leaves

räumen und Parks, Sportanlagen und Verkehrsknotenpunkten, Sakralbauten und Friedhöfen menschenleer.

Wenn die blaue Stunde längst vorbei ist und die astronomische Dämmerung das Zepter führt, wird es still in der großen Stadt. Vereinzelt erklingen noch Stimmen zwischen den Häuserzeilen, und auf den Hauptstraßen sammeln Taxis die letzten Nachtschwärmer ein. Dann dringen andere Geräusche an unser Ohr. Am Tiergarten das Rauschen der Blätter im Wind, in der Laubenkolonie das Quietschen des Scharniers einer offenen Pforte. Manchmal hört man den Schrei einer Katze oder das Maunzen eines Katers auf der Suche nach einem Liebesabenteuer. In den Hecken der Vorortsiedlungen rascheln Fuchs oder Marder, und das Plätschern des Weltkugelbrunnens hat am Breitscheidplatz die akustische Regie übernommen.

Menschen sieht man jetzt fast nur noch an den Hot Spots. Vor den Nordischen Botschaften werden die wachhabenden Polizisten in der ansonsten menschenleeren Rauchstraße wie Bekannte gegrüßt. Auf dem Gelände zwischen der Neuen Wache und dem Maxim Gorki Theater ist man ganz allein. Würde man tagsüber die nun dramatisch beleuchtete Rückseite der Neuen Wache überhaupt wahrnehmen? Nähme man sich am Nachmittag Zeit, um die nach Plänen von Karl Friedrich Schinkel gebaute klassizistische Fassade des Maxim Gorki gebührend zu bewundern, die nun, von zwei Doppellaternen angeleuchtet, ihr schönstes Gesicht zeigt? Und wenn man am Rand der Hufeisensiedlung die von Martin Wagner entworfene Wohnzeile an der Stavenhagener Straße mit ihren bastionsartig vortretenden halbrunden Treppenhäusern und den vorgelagerten Grünanlagen abschreitet, dann wähnt man sich in einer anderen Zeit. Oder einem anderen Ort: am Rand einer geheimnisvollen Burganlage, über die sich ein imposant bewölkter Himmel wölbt und deren Inneres man sich in phantastischen Bildern ausmalt.

Diese geheimnisvolle Unruhe im Zwielicht zwischen Mondschein und Straßenbeleuchtung, die fast gespenstische Farbe, die Berlin in der Dunkelheit annimmt, diese Melange aus fahlen Farben, schimmernden Fassaden, glänzenden Straßen und dunklen Parkanlagen, das alles habe ich auf meine Weise sichtbar zu machen versucht. Und glaube, dabei verstanden zu haben, dass Berlin in der Nacht zu einem anderen Leben erwacht. Mein Buch zeigt die Stadt in ihrem ganz eigenen ***Nachtleben***.

rustle in the breeze, in a garden colony the hinge of an open gate creaks. Sometimes you can hear the screech of a cat or the meowing of a tomcat out prowling in search of love. Foxes and weasels scavenge in the hedges of suburban housing estates and the splashing of the Weltkugel fountain on Breitscheidplatz has taken charge of the soundscape.

The only places where you can see any people are at the city's hot spots. The policemen on duty in front of the Nordic Embassies on the otherwise deserted Rauchstrasse are greeted like friends. But on the space between the Neue Wache and the Maxim Gorki Theatre you are quite alone. In the daytime would you notice the back of the Neue Wache that is now so dramatically illuminated?

Would you take the time in an afternoon to marvel with due admiration at Karl Friedrich Schinkel's classical façade of the Maxim Gorki Theatre?

And if you walk along the row of houses on Stavenhagener Strasse on the edge of the Hufeisensiedlung ('Horseshoe Estate'), with their bastion-shaped, semi-circular, protuberant stairwells designed by Martin Wagner, then you might imagine that you are in another time.

Or perhaps in another place – on the edge of the grounds of a secret castle beneath a grand and gloomy sky, whose interior you picture in fantastic images.

In my own way, I have tried to communicate that mysterious disquiet in the twilight between moonlight and streetlight, the almost ghostly colour that Berlin takes on in the dark, that melange of pallid colours, shimmering façades, gleaming streets and dark parks. And I think that in doing so, I have understood that after dusk Berlin awakes to another life. My book portrays the city in its own special Nightlife.

S-Bahnhof Friedrichstraße | Mitte

Friedrichstrasse S-Bahn Station | Mitte district

Theater des Westens | Charlottenburg
Theatre of the West | Charlottenburg district

Schaubühne am Lehniner Platz | Charlottenburg
Playhouse on Lehniner Platz | Charlottenburg district

Karl-Marx-Allee | Mitte
Karl-Marx-Allee | Mitte district

Karl-Marx-Allee | Mitte

Karl-Marx-Allee | Mitte district

Jacob-und-Wilhelm-Grimm-Zentrum | Mitte
Jacob and Wilhelm Grimm Centre | Mitte district

Jacob-und-Wilhelm-Grimm-Zentrum | Mitte
Jacob and Wilhelm Grimm Centre | Mitte district

Flensburger Löwe am Großen Wannsee | Zehlendorf
Flensburg Lion by the Great Wannsee lake | Zehlendorf district

Großer Wannsee | Zehlendorf

Great Wannsee lake | Zehlendorf district

Sammlung Boros im ehemaligen Reichsbahnbunker Friedrichstraße | Mitte

Boros Collection in the former Friedrichstrasse Imperial Railway bunker | Mitte district

Sammlung Boros im ehemaligen Reichsbahnbunker Friedrichstraße | Mitte

Boros Collection in the former Friedrichstrasse Imperial Railway bunker | Mitte district

Gebäude der Nordischen Botschaften | Tiergarten
Nordic Embassies building | Tiergarten district

Audimax der TU-Berlin | Charlottenburg
Main lecture hall of Berlin Technical University | Charlottenburg district

Kinder- und Jugendzirkus Cabuwazi auf dem Tempelhofer Feld | Tempelhof
Cabuwazi Children's and Youth Circus on Tempelhof airfield | Tempelhof district

Kinder- und Jugendzirkus Cabuwazi auf dem Tempelhofer Feld | Tempelhof
Cabuzawi Children's and Youth Circus on Tempelhof airfield | Tempelhof district

Deutsches Theater | Mitte

German National Theatre | Mitte district

Deutsches Theater | Mitte

German National Theatre | Mitte district

Stadion An der alten Försterei | Köpenick
Stadium at the Old Forester's House | Koepenick district

Stadion An der alten Försterei | Köpenick

Stadium at the Old Forester's House | Koepenick district

Bundesnachrichtendienst | Wedding
Federal Intelligence Service | Wedding district

Bundesnachrichtendienst | Wedding
Federal Intelligence Service | Wedding district

Alte Nationalgalerie | Mitte

Old National Gallery | Mitte district

Alte Nationalgalerie | Mitte
Old National Gallery | Mitte district

Ballhaus Berlin | Mitte

Berlin Dance Hall | Mitte district

Ballhaus Berlin | Mitte
Berlin Dance Hall | Mitte district

Bauhaus-Archiv Museum für Gestaltung | Tiergarten
Bauhaus Archive Design Museum | Tiergarten district

Ehemaliges Dynamo-Sporthotel und Kongresszentrum Konrad-Wolf-Straße, Ecke Weißenseer Weg | Lichtenberg

Former Dynamo-Sporthotel and Congress Centre on the corner of Konrad-Wolf-Strasse and Weissenseer Weg | Lichtenberg district

Flughafen Tegel | Reinickendorf
Tegel Airport | Reinickendorf district

Flughafen Tegel | Reinickendorf

Tegel Airport | Reinickendorf district

Botanischer Garten | Zehlendorf

Botanic Gardens | Zehlendorf district

Botanischer Garten | Zehlendorf

Botanic Gardens | Zehlendorf district

Bernauer Straße | Prenzlauer Berg

Bernauer Strasse | Prenzlauer Berg district

Bernauer Straße | Prenzlauer Berg

Bernauer Strasse | Prenzlauer Berg district

Uhlandstraße | Charlottenburg
Uhlandstrasse | Charlottenburg district

Bundesallee | Wilmersdorf
Bundesallee | Wilmersdorf district

Haus des Rundfunks am Hammarskjöldplatz | Charlottenburg

Broadcasting House on Hammarskjoeldplatz | Charlottenburg district

Penny-Discount und Hotel Ambiente Berlin City | Schöneberg

Penny discount store and Hotel Ambiente Berlin City | Schoeneberg district

Billardsalon in der Knesebeckstraße | Charlottenburg

Pool hall in Knesebeckstrasse | Charlottenburg district

Kugelbahn | Wedding
Skittle alley | Wedding district

Sowjetisches Ehrenmal | Tiergarten
Soviet War Memorial | Tiergarten district

Bismarck-Nationaldenkmal | Tiergarten

National Memorial to Bismarck | Tiergarten district

Burger King Restaurant im Berlin Pavillon | Tiergarten
Burger King Restaurant in the Berlin Pavillon | Tiergarten district

Burger King Restaurant im Berlin Pavillon | Tiergarten

Burger King Restaurant in the Berlin Pavillon | Tiergarten district

Altberliner Kneipe Wilhelm Hoeck | Charlottenburg
Old Berlin pub 'Wilhelm Hoeck' | Charlottenburg district

Altberliner Kneipe Wilhelm Hoeck | Charlottenburg

Old Berlin pub 'Wilhelm Hoeck' | Charlottenburg district

Walter-Benjamin-Platz | Charlottenburg
Walter-Benjamin-Platz | Charlottenburg district

Haus der Kulturen der Welt | Tiergarten
House of World Cultures | Tiergarten district

AUSSTELLUNG
13.4.–9.7.
NEOLITHISCHE KINDHEIT
KUNST IN EINER FALSCHEN GEGENWART, CA. 1930
HAUS DER KULTUREN DER WELT

Am Hohenzollernplatz | Wilmersdorf

Hohenzollernplatz | Wilmersdorf district

Kirche am Hohenzollernplatz | Wilmersdorf

Church on Hohenzollernplatz | Wilmersdorf district

Wartungshalle auf dem BVG-Betriebshof Lichtenberg | Lichtenberg
Maintenance hangar at the Berlin Transport depot in Lichtenberg | Lichtenberg district

BVG-Betriebshof | Lichtenberg
Berlin Transport depot | Lichtenberg district

BVG-Betriebshof Indira-Gandhi-Straße | Weißensee

Berlin Transport bus depot in Indira-Gandhi-Strasse | Weissensee district

Container-Lager am Standort von Zapf Umzüge | Neukölln

Container park at the Zapf Removal Company site | Neukoelln district

Dorfkirche Marienfelde | Tempelhof
Marienfelde Village Church | Tempelhof district

Gutshaus Marienfelde | Tempelhof

Marienfelde Manor House | Tempelhof district

Öffentliche Toilette am S- und U-Bahnhof Olympia Stadion | Charlottenburg

Public toilet at Olympic Stadium S-Bahn and Underground Station | Charlottenburg district

Steffi-Graf-Stadion des Lawn-Tennis-Turnier-Club Rot-Weiß am Hundekehlesee | Zehlendorf

Steffi Graf Stadium of the Rot-Weiss Lawn Tennis Tournament Club by Hundekehle Lake | Zehlendorf district

U-Bahnhof Kottbusser Tor | Kreuzberg

Kottbusser Tor Underground Station | Kreuzberg district

Kottbusser Tor | Kreuzberg

Kottbusser Tor | Kreuzberg district

Schloss Friedrichsfelde im Tierpark Berlin | Lichtenberg

Friedrichsfelde Palace in the Tierpark Berlin zoo | Lichtenberg district

Eisbärenfelsen im Tierpark Berlin | Lichtenberg

Polar bear enclosure in the Tierpark Berlin zoo | Lichtenberg district

Westhafen | Tiergarten

West Harbour | Tiergarten district

Westhafen | Tiergarten

West Harbour | Tiergarten district

eddyline.de
PINGUIN

U-Bahnhof Dahlem Dorf | Zehlendorf

Dahlem Dorf Underground Station | Zehlendorf district

Restaurant Alter Krug Dahlem | Zehlendorf

'Alter Krug' (Old Jug) restaurant in Dahlem | Zehlendorf district

Fußgängerunterführung am Messedamm | Charlottenburg

Pedestrian subway on Messedamm | Charlottenburg district

U-Bahnhof Klosterstraße | Mitte
Klosterstrasse Underground Station | Mitte district

Kant-Garagen | Charlottenburg

Kant Multi-Storey Car Park | Charlottenburg district

Kant-Garagen | Charlottenburg

Kant Multi-Storey Car Park | Charlottenburg district

Das Pallasseum, umgangssprachlich Sozialpalast, an der Pallasstraße | Schöneberg
The Pallasseum, known as the 'Social Palace', in Pallas Street | Schoeneberg district

Wohnhaus in der Fritz-Reuter-Allee | Neukölln
Apartment block in Fritz-Reuter-Allee | Neukoelln district

Von Martin Wagner entworfene Wohnzeile an der Stavenhagener Straße | Neukölln
Row of houses in Stavenhagener Strasse, designed by Martin Wagner | Neukoelln district

Hufeisensiedlung von Bruno Taut | Neukölln
'Horseshoe Estate' designed by Bruno Taut | Neukoelln district

Hauptbahnhof | Tiergarten

Central Rail Station | Tiergarten district

Hauptbahnhof | Tiergarten

Central Rail Station | Tiergarten district

Bahnhof Berlin Alexanderplatz | Mitte
Berlin Alexanderplatz Station | Mitte district

Künstlerhaus Bethanien | Kreuzberg

Bethanien contemporary arts centre | Kreuzberg district

Crêperie in der Kantstraße | Charlottenburg

Crêperie in Kantstrasse | Charlottenburg district

Hotel Riu Plaza Berlin | Schöneberg

Hotel Riu Plaza Berlin | Schoeneberg district

Die Nacht über Berlin im Zeiss-Großplanetarium | Prenzlauer Berg
The night sky above Berlin in the Zeiss Planetarium | Prenzlauer Berg district

Zeiss-Großplanetarium | Prenzlauer Berg
Zeiss Planetarium | Prenzlauer Berg district

Mercedes-Benz Arena | Friedrichshain
Mercedes Benz Arena | Friedrichshain district

Mercedes-Benz Arena | Friedrichshain
Mercedes Benz Arena | Friedrichshain district

Hochbunker Pallasstraße | Schöneberg

The Hochbunker in Pallasstrasse | Schoeneberg district

Milchbar im Funkhaus Berlin | Treptow

Milk Bar in Berlin Recording Studios | Treptow district

Villa in der Limonenstraße | Zehlendorf

Mansion in Limonenstrasse | Zehlendorf district

Villa in der Limonenstraße | Zehlendorf

Mansion in Limonenstrasse | Zehlendorf district

W. Michael Blumenthal Akademie | Kreuzberg
W. Michael Blumenthal Academy | Kreuzberg district

Jüdisches Museum Berlin | Kreuzberg
Jewish Museum Berlin | Kreuzberg district

Tankstelle am Hotel Avus | Charlottenburg
Service station at Hotel Avus | Charlottenburg district

Hotel Avus | Charlottenburg
Hotel Avus | Charlottenburg district

Amerikanisches Restaurant am Winterfeldtplatz | Schöneberg
American Restaurant on Winterfeldtplatz | Schoeneberg district

Amerikanisches Restaurant am Ludwigkirchplatz | Wilmersdorf
American Restaurant on Ludwigkirchplatz | Wilmersdorf district

Hotel Oderberger | Prenzlauer Berg
Hotel Oderberger | Prenzlauer Berg district

Hotel Oderberger | Prenzlauer Berg
Hotel Oderberger | Prenzlauer Berg district

Palais in der Kulturbrauerei | Prenzlauer Berg

Palais in the Kulturbrauerei – event location | Prenzlauer Berg district

Konopke's Imbiß | Prenzlauer Berg

Konopke's sausage stand | Prenzlauer Berg district

Haubentaucher – Sommerclub in der Revaler Straße | Friedrichshain
Great crested grebe – Summer Club in Revaler Strasse | Friedrichshain district

Station Berlin – Stage One der re:publica | Kreuzberg

Station Berlin – Stage One of the re:publica (annual congress) | Kreuzberg district

Volksbühne | Mitte

People's Playhouse | Mitte district

Maxim Gorki Theater | Mitte

Maxim Gorki Theatre | Mitte district

Rückseite der Neuen Wache Unter den Linden | Mitte
Back of the Neue Wache (War Memorial) on Unter den Linden | Mitte district

Denkmal für die ermordeten Juden Europas | Mitte
Memorial to the murdered Jews of Europe | Mitte district

Am Potsdamer Platz | Mitte

Potsdamer Platz | Mitte district

BahnTower am Potsdamer Platz | Mitte
RailTower on Potsdamer Platz | Mitte district

Leipziger Platz | Mitte

Leipziger Platz | Mitte district

Restaurantschiff Alte Liebe an der Havel | Charlottenburg

'Alte Liebe' restaurant boat on the Havel River | Charlottenburg district

Neubau Cube Berlin am Hauptbahnhof | Tiergarten

The new 'Cube Berlin' at the Central Rail Station | Tiergarten district

Spittelkolonnaden an der Leipziger Straße | Mitte
Spittel Colonnades on Leipziger Strasse | Mitte district

Bundeskanzleramt | Tiergarten
Federal Chancellery | Tiergarten district

Greifenskulptur an der Moltkebrücke | Tiergarten
Griffin sculpture on Moltke Bridge | Tiergarten district

Bar in der Fasanenstraße 37 | Wilmersdorf
Bar at 37 Fasanenstrasse | Wilmersdorf district

Winterbild in einem Gartenhaus der Fasanenstraße | Wilmersdorf
Winter in a Fasanenstrasse garden house | Wilmersdorf district

Sommerbild in einem Gartenhaus der Fasanenstraße | Wilmersdorf

Summer in a Fasanenstrasse garden house | Wilmersdorf district

Kindergarten am Fasanenplatz | Wilmersdorf
Kindergarten on Fasanenplatz | Wilmersdorf district

Luxuriöses Neubauvorhaben Fasanenstraße 63 | Wilmersdorf

Luxury new development at 63 Fasanenstrasse | Wilmersdorf district

Neubau Fasanenstraße 63 | Wilmersdorf

New building at 63 Fasanenstrasse | Wilmersdorf district

Schlangenbrücke im Tiergarten | Tiergarten

Schlangenbruecke (Snake Bridge) in Tiergarten Park | Tiergarten district

Späti in der Uhlandstraße | Wilmersdorf

Late night shop in Uhlandstrasse | Wilmersdorf district

Parksiedlung Spruch | Neukölln
Spruch housing community | Neukoelln district

Blick auf die Pfaueninsel | Zehlendorf
View of Peacock Island | Zehlendorf district

»Café Achteck« am Rüdesheimer Platz | Wilmersdorf

'Café Achteck' (historic octagonal public urinal) on Rudesheimer Platz | Wilmersdorf district

City Toilette Am Lustgarten | Mitte

City Toilet at the Lustgarten (Pleasure Garden) | Mitte district

Laubenpieperidylle am Britzer Garten | Neukölln
Idyll for allotment gardeners at Britz Gardens | Neukoelln district

Laube am S-Bahnhof Westkreuz | Charlottenburg

Garden colony at Westkreuz S-Bahn Station | Charlottenburg district

Westberliner City | Charlottenburg
West Berlin City | Charlottenburg district

Westberliner City | Charlottenburg
West Berlin City | Charlottenburg district

aktivschuh
Tauentzienstr.5

Brandmauer am S-Bahnhof Savignyplatz | Charlottenburg
Fire wall at Savignyplatz S-Bahn Station | Charlottenburg district

S-Bahnhof Westkreuz | Charlottenburg

Westkreuz S-Bahn Station | Charlottenburg district

Max Brown Hotel in der Uhlandstraße | Wilmersdorf

Max Brown Hotel in Uhlandstrasse | Wilmersdorf district

Max Brown Hotel in der Uhlandstraße | Wilmersdorf

Max Brown Hotel in Uhlandstrasse | Wilmersdorf district

Lobby des Hotels Grand Hyatt | Mitte
Grand Hyatt hotel lobby | Mitte district

Bar des Hotels Sofitel in der Augsburger Straße | Charlottenburg

Sofitel hotel bar in Augsburger Strasse | Charlottenburg district

2FREE SPACE – Metallskulptur von Dirk Bell in der Otto-Suhr-Allee | Charlottenburg

2FREE SPACE – Metal sculpture by Dirk Bell on Otto-Suhr-Allee | Charlottenburg district

Gebäude der Deutschen Bank am Ernst-Reuter-Platz | Charlottenburg
Deutsche Bank building on Ernst-Reuter-Platz | Charlottenburg district

Volksfest auf der Straße des 17. Juni | Tiergarten

Fun Fair on Strasse des 17. Juni | Tiergarten district

Straße des 17. Juni | Tiergarten

Strasse des 17. Juni | Tiergarten district

Ausstellungshalle des Deutschen Historischen Museums von I.M. Pei | Mitte
Exhibition Hall of the German History Museum, designed by I.M. Pei | Mitte district

Berliner Dom | Mitte
Berlin Cathedral | Mitte district

Corbusierhaus | Charlottenburg
Corbusier building | Charlottenburg district

Olympia-Stadion | Charlottenburg

Olympic Stadium | Charlottenburg district

Blick auf die Havelinsel Lindwerder | Zehlendorf
View of Lindwerder island in the Havel River | Zehlendorf district

Berliner Congress Centrum | Mitte
Berlin Congress Centre | Mitte district

bcc

Am S-Bahnhof Olympia-Stadion | Charlottenburg

Olympic Stadium S-Bahn station | Charlottenburg district

Am S-Bahnhof Olympia-Stadion | Charlottenburg

Olympic Stadium S-Bahn station | Charlottenburg district

Fernsehturm am Alexanderplatz | Mitte
Television tower on Alexanderplatz | Mitte district

Siegessäule | Tiergarten
Victory Column | Tiergarten district

Volkswagen Universitätsbibliothek der TU Berlin in der Fasanenstraße | Charlottenburg
Volkswagen University Library of the Berlin Technical University in Fasanenstrasse | Charlottenburg district

Sphinx der Königin Hatschepsut in Dussmann Das Kulturkaufhaus | Mitte

Queen Hatschepsut Sphinx in Dussmann Culture Store | Mitte district

Schleichers Buchhandlung in Dahlem-Dorf | Zehlendorf

Schleicher's bookshop in Dahlem-Dorf (Dahlem village) | Zehlendorf district

Die Marga Schoeller Bücherstube in der Knesebeckstraße | Charlottenburg
The Marga Schoeller bookshop in Knesebeckstrasse | Charlottenburg district

Die »Kommode« – Juristische Fakultät der Humboldt-Universität | Mitte
The 'Chest of Drawers' – Law Faculty of Humboldt University | Mitte district

Niederländische Botschaft | Mitte

Embassy of the Netherlands | Mitte district

Internationales Congress Centrum mit Funkturm | Charlottenburg
International Congress Centre with radio tower | Charlottenburg district

Messe Berlin am Hammarskjöldplatz | Charlottenburg

Berlin Exhibition Centre on Hammarskjoeldplatz | Charlottenburg district

Aral-Tankstelle Holzmarktstraße | Friedrichshain

Aral service station on Holzmarktstrasse | Friedrichshain district

Blick von der Kronprinzenbrücke | Mitte

View from Kronprinzenbrucke (Crown Prince Bridge) | Mitte district

Freilichtbühne auf dem Gutshof Britz | Neukölln

Open-air theatre on the Britz manor estate | Neukoelln district

Neukölln Museum auf dem Gutshof Britz | Neukölln

Neukoelln Museum on the Britz manor estate | Neukoelln district

Schloss Britz | Neukölln
Schloss Britz manor house | Neukoelln district

Richardplatz in Rixdorf | Neukölln
Richardplatz in Rixdorf | Neukoelln district

Gärtnerei am Friedhof Heerstraße | Charlottenburg

Nursery at the Heerstrasse cemetery | Charlottenburg district

Grab von Loriot auf dem Friedhof Heerstraße | Charlottenburg
Grave of the comedian Loriot in Heerstrasse cemetery | Charlottenburg district

Museum für Naturkunde | Mitte
Natural History Museum | Mitte district

Museum für Naturkunde | Mitte

Natural History Museum | Mitte district

Berliner Medizinhistorisches Museum der Charité | Mitte

Berlin History of Medicine Museum at the Charité Hospital | Mitte district

Supermarkt in der Uhlandstraße | Wilmersdorf
Supermarket in Uhlandstrasse | Wilmersdorf district

Linienstraße | Mitte
Linienstrasse | Mitte district

Wohnhaus Von-der-Heydt-Straße 1 | Tiergarten

Apartment block at 1, Von-der-Heydt Strasse | Tiergarten district

Restaurant Tunnel-Eck am Rand der Laubenpieper-Kolonie Schleusenland | Charlottenburg
'Tunnel-Eck' Restaurant on the edge of the Schleusenland garden colony | Charlottenburg district

Ziegenhof in der Danckelmannstraße | Charlottenburg
Goat farm in Danckelmannstrasse | Charlottenburg district

S-Bahnhof Potsdamer Platz | Mitte

Potsdamer Platz S-Bahn Station | Mitte district

Altes Museum Unter den Linden | Mitte

Altes Museum (Old Museum) on Unter den Linden | Mitte district

Paul-Löbe-Haus | Tiergarten

Paul Loebe House | Tiergarten district

Regierungsviertel | Tiergarten

Government district | Tiergarten district

The Feuerle Collection im ehemaligen Kommunikationsbunker | Kreuzberg
The Feuerle Collection in a former telecommunication bunker | Kreuzberg district

The Feuerle Collection im ehemaligen Kommunikationsbunker | Kreuzberg

The Feuerle Collection in a former telecommunication bunker | Kreuzberg district

ARTIST HOMES im ehemaligen Kontrollbunker der Luftabwehr | Wilmersdorf

ARTIST HOMES in a former Luftwaffe air defence bunker | Wilmersdorf district

Foto-Ausstellung von Jan R. Tyler in der Galerie Schöne Weide | Treptow

Photo exhibition by Jan R. Tyler in the Schoene Weide Gallery | Treptow district

Zementwerk Berlin | Lichtenberg
Berlin Cement Works | Lichtenberg district

Baustelle Kudamm-Karree in der Uhlandstraße | Charlottenburg

The Ku-damm Karree building site in Uhlandstrasse | Charlottenburg district

Villa am Majakowskiring | Pankow
Mansion on Majakowskiring | Pankow district

Das Shell-Haus am Reichpietschufer | Tiergarten

The Shell Building on Reichpietschufer | Tiergarten district

LIGHT DELUXE – Kronleuchter in der Gitschiner Straße | Kreuzberg

LIGHT DELUXE – Chandeliers in Gitscheiner Strasse | Kreuzberg district

Waldgott-Skulptur des Berliner Künstlers F.M. Schreiber in der Christstraße | Charlottenburg

Silvan God sculpture by Berlin artist F.M. Schreiber in Christstrasse | Charlottenburg district

Westberliner City zwischen Kurfürstendamm und Kantstraße | Charlottenburg
West Berlin City between Kurfuerstendamm and Kantstrasse | Charlottenburg district

Voliere im Hof des Neuen Kranzler Ecks | Charlottenburg

Aviary in the courtyard of the Neues Kranzler Eck | Charlottenburg district

St. Hedwigs-Kathedrale Berlin | Mitte
St Hedwig's Cathedral Berlin | Mitte district

St.-Thomas-Kirche | Kreuzberg
St Thomas's Church | Kreuzberg district

Zoologischer Garten Berlin | Charlottenburg
Berlin Zoological Gardens | Charlottenburg district

Zoologischer Garten Berlin | Charlottenburg
Berlin Zoological Gardens | Charlottenburg district

Berghain | Friedrichshain

Berghain nightclub | Friedrichshain district

Zoo Palast | Charlottenburg
Zoo Palast cinema | Charlottenburg district

Denkmal für die im Nationalsozialismus verfolgten Homosexuellen | Tiergarten

Memorial to the Homosexuals Persecuted under the National Socialist Regime | Tiergarten district

Kueka-Stein aus Venezuela – Teil des Kunstprojektes »Global Stone« | Tiergarten

Kueka Stone from Venezuela – part of the 'Global Stone' art project | Tiergarten district

DANK

Ohne die tatkräftige Unterstützung vieler Menschen hätte eine große Zahl von Fotografien nicht in dieses Buch aufgenommen werden können. Sie haben Anregungen gegeben, Zugänge ermöglicht oder Genehmigungen erteilt – nicht nur, aber insbesondere in und für Räume, die während der Nacht für die Öffentlichkeit nicht zugänglich sind, in denen ich zumeist ganz allein in Ruhe fotografieren konnte. Ihnen allen möchte ich an dieser Stelle durch die Nennung ihres Namens auf der folgenden Seite herzlich für ihre großzügige Unterstützung danken.

Vor allem aber gilt mein Dank Rolf-Peter Baacke, der mich oft bei meinen nächtlichen Streifzügen durch die Stadt begleitet hat und mir mit Rat und Tat zur Seite stand. Ferner danke ich herzlich meiner Frau Ruth Klinkenberg, die mein Projekt in jeder Hinsicht verständnisvoll unterstützt hat.

ACKNOWLEDGEMENTS

A large number of photographs in this book could not have been taken without the active support of many people. They provided suggestions, facilitated access or granted permission – not only, but particularly in and for places which are not accessible to the public at night and where I was usually able to take photographs in peace and alone. I would like to take this opportunity to thank them all sincerely for their generous support; their names are listed on the following page.

Above all, I am grateful to Rolf-Peter Baacke who often accompanied me on my nocturnal tours through the city and gave me advice and help. I would also like to warmly thank my wife, Ruth Klinkenberg, who sympathetically supported my project in every way.

Türkan Arikan *(Hotel de Rome)*
Mohammed Bartout *(Burger King)*
Paul Berschick *(re:publica)*
Christof Blaesius *(Ballhaus Berlin)*
Marco Boerner *(Ballhaus Berlin)*
David Boldt *(Funkhaus Berlin)*
Christian Boros *(Boros Foundation)*
Julia Claren *(Dussmann Das Kulturkaufhaus)*
Carsten Colmorgen
Andreas Degkwitz *(Grimm-Zentrum)*
Katrin Dittrich *(Alte Försterei)*
Christine Drawer *(Deutsches Theater)*
Birgit Fäth *(BVG)*
Désiré Feuerle *(The Feuerle Collection)*
Falk Flach
Deborah Frank *(Grand Hyatt Berlin)*
Michael Fritsch *(Galerie Schöne Weide)*
Dirk Gädecke *(Kantgaragenpalast)*
Isa Gengenbach
Stefan Gotthold *(Zeiss Großplanetarium | Stiftung Planetarium Berlin)*
Philine Hachmeister *(Zoo + Tierpark Berlin)*
Michael Hapka *(Mercedes-Benz Arena)*
Jan Hegemann *(Raue LLP)*
Gesche Hohlstein *(Botanischer Garten)*
Ulrich Hopp
Tim Florian Horn *(Zeiss Großplanetarium | Stiftung Planetarium Berlin)*
Moritz Indenhuck *(Lindenpartners)*
Verena Jaeschke *(Hotel Oderberger Berlin)*
Gregor Jagodic *(Slowenisches Kulturzentrum Berlin)*
Jong-Ha Kim *(Artist Homes)*
Kilian Kissling
Shino Kobayashi *(The Feuerle Collection)*
Simone Koch *(Botanischer Garten)*
Karl Köckenberger *(Kinder- und Jugendzirkus Cabuwazi)*
Katrin Konst *(Botschaft des Königreichs der Niederlande in Berlin)*
Juliet Kothe *(Boros Foundation)*
Katja Krause *(Grimm-Zentrum)*
Axel Krumrey *(Zapf Umzüge)*
Achim Lahrem
Josefin Langer *(BVG)*
Heinz-Werner Lawo
Daniel Lente *(Haubentaucher)*
Marcel Manasse *(Billard International)*
Daniele Maruca *(The Feuerle Collection)*
Uli Mayer-Johanssen
Sibel Özkilic *(Dussmann Das Kulturkaufhaus)*
Maria Ostberg *(Haubentaucher)*
Oliver Ramm
Michael Reimann *(Westhafen)*
Monique Ruhe *(Botschaft des Königreichs der Niederlande in Berlin)*
Uwe Schenk *(BVG)*
Martina Scherpner *(Freyer Marktforschung)*
Monika Schindler *(Mercedes-Benz Arena)*
Johanna Schirm *(Max Brown Hotels)*
Jessica Schmidt *(Kugelbahn)*
Thomas Schnalke *(Berliner Medizinhistorisches Museum der Charité)*
Beate Schneider *(Deutsche Bahn AG)*
Marc Schneppensief *(Berliner Medizinhistorisches Museum der Charité)*
Friedrich Michael Schreiber *(FriedrichsLust)*
Franziska Schultze *(Zeiss Großplanetarium | Stiftung Planetarium Berlin)*
Stephanie Schwarzer *(Freyer Marktforschung)*
Grit Sperschneider *(Kulturbrauerei)*
Gesine Steiner *(Museum für Naturkunde)*
Marko Tobjinski *(Wilhelm Hoeck)*
Katharina Tollkühn *(Grimm-Zentrum)*
Jan K. Tyrel
Dominique Vockeradt *(Sofitel Berlin)*
Stefan Voelker *(Nah&Gut)*
Ute Warbein
Markus Zoecke *(LTTC »Rot-Weiß«)*

© Johanna Hahn

DER FOTOGRAF

Detlef Bluhm, geboren 1954 in Berlin, studierte Religionspädagogik und Theologie, landete beruflich aber im Buch- und Verlagswesen. Seit 1992 ist er Geschäftsführer des Börsenvereins des Deutschen Buchhandels, Landesverband Berlin-Brandenburg. Er hat zahlreiche Bücher veröffentlicht, darunter Romane und kulturgeschichtliche Sachbücher, die in insgesamt sechs Sprachen übersetzt worden sind. Als Fotograf porträtierte er zuletzt das Dorf Sandberg und die Stadt Gersfeld in der Rhön.

THE PHOTOGRAPHER

Detlef Bluhm, born in 1954 in Berlin, studied Religious Education and Theology but then followed a career in books and publishing. Since 1992 he has been heading up the regional office of the German Publishers and Booksellers Association in Berlin-Brandenburg. He has had numerous books published, including novels and historico-cultural nonfiction books, which have been translated into a total of six languages. As a photographer he has recently portrayed the village of Sandberg and the town of Gersfeld in the Rhoen Mountains.